Prison Days

Book 4

True Diary Entries
by a Maximum-Security Prison Officer

September, 2018

Copyright © 2019 by Simon King

All rights reserved. This book or any portion thereof may not be reproduced or used in any manner whatsoever without the express written permission of the publisher except for the use of brief quotations in a book review or scholarly journal.
First Printing: 2019

By Simon King

Prison Days June

Prison Days July

Prison Days August

COMING SOON

The Final Alibi

Introduction

Welcome to the fourth instalment of Prison Days. I must say that each month, I wonder whether I will have enough material to complete another book and every month the prisoners come through for me. Come through in spades, in fact. Should I ever doubt them? And as long as people buy them, I'm more than happy to keep sharing the insane behaviour that seems to be a part of life behind the walls.

But two things have really turned my experiences upside down this month and I don't think life can ever be the same. The first thing that really made my month was the return of an old friend. You read about him in the June edition of Prison Days and I was very happy to see him return.

The second event that left the prison staff reeling in shock was the loss of one of our own and is something that I will reveal to you within the following pages. But I will say the shock from losing one of our own, is one that will never diminish.

So, are you ready for another journey behind the razor wire? Ready to hear the stories from beyond the walls?

Units

All the units in the prison are named after rivers and consist of management, step-down management, protection and main stream.

Management Units

Units that are predominately single occupancy out of necessity or punishment and have 23-hour lock ins. Prisoners only receive a one hour run out from their cell.
Murray North and South are the Management Units.

Step Down Management

Units that are a step down from the 23-hour lock down. Prisoners are given extra run-outs throughout the day but limited to around 3 to 4 hours. Some prisoners can mix and have joint run-outs.
Goulburn East and West are the Step-Down Management Units.

Protection Units

Yarra North and South, Loddon North and South, Glenelg East and West

Main Stream Units

Thomson East and West, Tambo East and West, Campaspe, Avoca, Maribyrnong,

Other Areas

Kitchen, Laundry, Medical Wing, Reception

Some Prison Terms

- Air- Raiding- Yelling or abusing someone loudly in the middle of a unit.

- Billet- A prisoner who is assigned a particular duty in the unit, on a daily basis, for a weekly pay packet. They hold the position until they are either transferred out, sacked or quit.

- Bone Yard- A protection unit. Protection prisoners are also known as Boners.

- Booted- To hide something in the anus

- Boss- What prisoners call an officer. It began early last century, is a reverse insult and means "Sorry Son of a Bitch"

- Brew- A cup of Coffee or Tea

- Brasco- Toilet or brasco roll is toilet paper.

- Bronze Up- To cover ones' self in faeces.

- Bunk- A prisoner's bed.

- Canteen- A prisoner's weekly shopping or shopping items.

- Cellie- A cellmate

- Chook Pen- A fenced-in area attached to a unit for prisoners to walk around in. Approximately 15m by 15m depending on which unit. Management units have multiple chook pens as prisoners have individual run outs throughout the day.

- Co-ee- A prisoner's co-accused

- Crook- How officers refer to inmates

- Dog- Someone who informs on another prisoner.
- Greens or Greys- Prisoner's prison uniform.
- Rock Spider- A paedophile.
- Screw- How inmates refer to officers.
- Shiv- home-made knife or blade.
- Slash Up- To self-harm
- The T.O.'s- Tactical Officers, that are highly trained and armed with batons and O.C. spray.
- Trap- A small latch in a cell door that can be lowered to allow access. It is normally either half way up or three quarters of the way up the cell door.

Codes

- Alpha- Officer needs assistance, Officer emergency
- Bravo- Lock down of Unit
- Charlie- Lock down of prison
- Delta- Fire
- Echo- Escape
- Foxtrot- Fight, Prisoner on Prisoner
- Mike- Medical emergency

Saturday, September 1

Was called in for overtime and to be honest, it's a great way to start the month, with a few extra bucks in next week's pay. I had a choice of several areas but decided to work in Loddon South. It's a protection unit and one that houses quite a number of loud, obnoxious crooks that, if you were to put a label on them, I would call painful. A large number of them are in protection due to drug debts which they owe to gangs within the prison. Others are there because they have given up information on prisoners, while a few are there simply because they fear the main stream units and have taken measures to ensure a move to protection.

While some protection units house paedophiles and mainly sex offenders, other units will house no sex offenders, their populations made up entirely of what main stream prisoners call "Rats". These rats are those who will share information with officers and move into a cushy protection unit. As an officer, I can tell you that there is very little difference between a non-sexual offender protection unit and a main stream unit. There are plenty of assaults, rapes, murders, standovers and smuggling that makes me wonder why some crooks will go to such extreme lengths to gain access to protection. It makes very little sense and yet it's a never-ending cycle.

The unit smells of mouldy rubbish as I walk in through the airlock. It's quiet as everybody is still locked down. Three officers are standing in the officer's station and wave at me as I enter. I wave back at them and take my belongings into the staff room where I put my lunch in the fridge and stow my bag in the cupboard.

I head back to the station and greet the 3 officers. Robert Nixon, Jason Smith and Tom Grady are all hunched over one of the unit logs. After shaking hands with each of them, I crane my neck to see what they are so engrossed in. It turns out to be the handover log, a book that is filled out by the previous day's staff. It is supposed to be filled out each evening, especially when specific events need to be highlighted to incoming staff and it appears that a significant event took place in the early evening. It must have happened just after I knocked off from duty the previous day because I didn't hear anything by the time I walked out.

There had been a significant assault in the unit; 3 prisoners attacking 1 other. All 3 were armed with shivs and attacked the victim in the open unit, visible to everyone. The entire incident had been captured on cctv and would provide pretty conclusive evidence when the time came. The victim had been taken to hospital, where he remains. The 3 attackers have been transferred to the management units and will be interviewed by police throughout the day. Both Robert and Jason were in the adjoining unit the previous night and had rushed in to help lock the unit down. Based on what they were saying, there was a lot of blood that had to be cleaned up. I listened as the 2 told us their war story with enthusiasm. It sounded scary and I understood their eagerness to share.

As I have mentioned before, normal officers do not carry weapons of any kind. We do not carry batons, or firearms or even pepper spray. You may think that a bit crazy considering the environment we work in but then you'd be forgiven for not remembering the most important part; the prisoners outnumber us at around 20 or 30 to 1. It would take very little effort for a group to overpower an officer and take their weapons. Although extreme, keeping weapons of any type away from prisoners is common practice. And as we all know; prisoners already have access to enough weapons of their own making without us adding to them. Some officers struggle to safely hang on to their security swipe cards long enough without losing them; I shudder at the thought of giving them weapons, as well.

Just then, the radio comes alive as control calls for morning count. Tom and Jason grab the muster sheet and begin going trap to trap to conduct our count while Robert checks his emails. The phone rings and I answer it. It's Thelma who is in the dispensary and asks whether I could send the unit's methadones to her once count is called correct. I agree and hang up.

The boys return to the station and once the numbers are added up, call the number in to control. Minutes later, the count is called correct and I make my way to the top tier to unlock our prisoners. It's a quick process of inserting the key, twisting the handle open and twisting the key back, thereby unlocking the door without actually opening the cell door. The top tier takes about 5 minutes and when I'm done, return to the station.

Sleepy heads begin to emerge from their cells, each heading to a specific spot in the unit. Most make a sprint for the kitchenette, grabbing their bread and lining up for a go at the toasters. There are several and each is a 4-slicer, increasing the speed of each prisoner's breakfast. There is a calm atmosphere in the unit but all of us know that things can kick off in a split second and remain vigilant as we each begin a required task.

Jason heads for the door as I announce morning methadone's to make their way to the airlock. Being a protection unit, every move has to be escorted by an officer which means one of us has to accompany the required prisoner to wherever they are needed throughout the prison. Some officers see this as a bad thing; I, however, love the idea of not being stuck in a unit all day. It can get pretty stale, sitting in a station with a bunch of guys for 12 hours. Getting the occasional escape means fresh air, a bit of exercise and above all, a break from the non-stop barrage of unit noise, which can include endless questions and requests from needy prisoners.

24 prisoners leave the unit with Jason and once the doors close, their excitement now out of the common area, the unit quietens

considerably. I check my emails and once finish, check out the list of random cell searches we have to do. There are 3 for us, allocated at random and I check the cell numbers against the muster. All 3 seem to be pretty straightforward crooks and I wave the list at Tom.

"Fancy getting your hands dirty?" I ask and he nods. We head off to the first cell and knock on the door. It's not that we need permission to enter, it's just seen as a small bit of courtesy if the prisoner is in the middle of a toilet break or something. We wait a second then open the door with a key. It's empty and I turn around to scan the unit for its owner. He isn't around and think he's probably off to the gym. Tom and I go in and immediately begin to search things. It's not like you see in the movies, where everything is upended and thrown on the floor, then trampled to bits. We take our time, ensuring we not only pay attention to the finer details, but also to avoid needle-stick injuries. The last thing either of us wants, is to be stuck by a real or make-shift needle that's just been used to inject drugs.

Needle-stick injuries are probably one of the most common injuries for an officer to get while on duty. It can come as easily as reaching into a dark place where you can't see, or sliding your fingers under edges of a bunk or shelf. Once you are stuck by a needle, the wait to see whether you are infected by a disease is 3 months. Think about that for a moment. 3 months of not knowing whether you have aids or hepatitis etc. And while you wait those 3 months out, there's no kissing your wife or husband; there's no intimacy with your partner; there's no kissing your children. You are anxiously awaiting the results for 12 longs weeks. I have never personally suffered a needle-stick injury and (touch wood), hope I never do.

Tom takes the clothing shelves, picking up each piece, shaking it out, then roughly refolds each piece and returns it to the shelf. Socks are unfolded; books are opened and the pages flicked through. Magazines are checked thoroughly and, as Tom is about to discover, can be a great hiding place for another sort of contraband.

There is a pile of magazines on a shelf above the clothing and Tom takes them down. Maybe half a dozen or so car mags are put o the small table and he begins to flick through them, one at a time. The first 5 don't reveal anything, but in the sixth, he hits pay dirt. The first few pages on either end are nothing special yet, hidden amongst the inner-most pages are torn out pages of hardcore porn. The porn has been ripped out of another magazine, then hidden amongst the pages of the car magazine. There are almost two dozen pictures showing everything from anal sex to blowjobs and beyond. It may not be considered as much on the outside, but in here, it's pure gold. The porn could be rented out for a night to fellow prisoners for drugs or favours, or even smuggled to a sex offender's unit for a time. Sex offenders would pay big money, real money, for this type of stuff.

"Great find," I say to Tom as he confiscates the magazine. We finish our search and find no other contraband. We exit the cell a short time later and head for the next, one on the upper level almost directly above the first. The door is open and the owner inside. It's Max Turner, a small-time crook in for parole breach. He has extensive drug debts and his appearance is enough to tell you that he's a full-blown junkie. This is probably the biggest cue for my partner and I because a junkie's cell can be filled with real and make-shift needles.

Once we've conducted our strip search and find nothing on his person, Tom and I commence our search. It doesn't take us long to find our first bit of contraband. There's an old plastic coffee jar on the top shelf and it's filled with pens; the clear variety as they are the only type allowed. This strikes me as odd considering there is no paper, no books and no other hint of reading or writing material. A jar filled with pens just looks out of place and as soon as we shake the pens on to the bed, we find several with needles hidden inside the plastic ink reservoirs. We find 7 in total and carefully place them back into the jar and remove the lot.

There's nothing else found inside the cell and we move to the next one, just 3 doors down. It's also occupied, but by 2 prisoners. We knock on the door then open it to find one on his knees in front of the other one who's sitting on the bunk. The sitter has his erection sticking straight up at attention, the saliva from the first prisoner running down its shaft. The one on his knees is already getting to his feet, his face a glowing beacon of embarrassment, while the other pulls his trackpants back up with a wide grin. For some, embarrassment does not come easy.

"Sorry boys, search time," I said and we strip each of them in turn, finding nothing out of order. Once they exit, we commence with the search and although thorough, find nothing out of place.

Once we get back to the officer's station, both Tom and I write reports for each of the cells, bagging and tagging the evidence, then notifying the supervisor. It isn't long before lunchtime count is called and, with nothing exciting happening, it passes without incident. The afternoon isn't really anything too interesting. If you've read the previous chapters of this series, then you already know the procedures that occupy the afternoon. Everything runs smoothly and the afternoon glides by. The only small bit of excitement is when the owner of the first cell returns, a crook who'd actually been at work for the day in one of the factories. He heads to his cell and by the time he reaches it, I've caught up to him to give him the bad news on his porn. He's a long-termer and an experienced prisoner. He doesn't show his disappointment, only a grin to try and play the loss down. He enters his cell and closes the door once I finish talking to him. As I walk away, I hear the dull thud as he punches his wall, clearly upset about the loss.

As we walk out a while later, I remind myself of the importance of reminding one's self of the little things that matter during the shift; like watching out for the needles. Sometimes it's the small pricks that can ruin your whole day.

Today has been a good day.

Sunday, September 2

Another overtime shift for me, which means a nice chunk of spare change in my pay packet this week. I'm asked to work in the medical wing and I look forward to a quiet day like it usually is. Although whenever I enter the unit, I still smell the overpowering stench of Robert Coleman (see August Edition), the memories of that day firmly entrenched into my brain. But the stench of shit is not what greets me as I open the inner door to the unit. I'm happy to see Thelma and Vincent (both from August Edition), both great officers to work with, and I know that for the most part, it should be a good day. They tell me that Doris Reading is doing a cook up and should be ready shortly. I slap my head, realizing that I forgot that it was Sunday.

I put my things away, then head to the kitchen to find Doris busy cooking a feast on 2 electric frypans and 2 sandwich presses. I give her a hug then hand her a tenner for my share of the food. She refuses it and I thank her with a kiss on the cheek which makes her blush a little. She doesn't look 62 and the blushing colour in her cheeks makes her look about 40. I head back to the officer's station and chat to the two about usual things. We only have one S3 in an observation cell and he's been very compliant. Sometimes, the suicide watches use threats to kill themselves as ways to bail from a unit. They become almost immediately compliant once they are given a suicide rating and put into an obso cell. I can see him sitting on his bunk as I check the CCTV monitor. He appears to be reading a book and sipping a coffee.

Shortly after, the four of us are also sipping coffee and eating bacon and egg rolls. The smell is amazing and Thelma even brought some delicious cloudy apple juice to wash it all down. It's a highlight of what turns out to be just an ordinary day of checks and escorts as we walk beside the nurses as they conduct their hourly rounds. A couple of times, patients vent their frustration when being woken for a jab here and a finger prick there, but overall, it's a pretty decent way to pocket some extra money on pay day. Rather than bore you with less than interesting stuff, I'll just tell you that it was a good Sunday and a great day to walk out of when we finally did 12 or so hours later.

Today, was a good day.

Monday, September 3

Rostered day off.

Tuesday, September 4

I come in and am directed to the kitchen for a couple of days. One of the normal staff members has taken some overdue annual leave and I get to fill in. It can be a great place to work, especially considering there's a very good kick-back; Food. I can already smell the first kick-back as soon as I walk through the door, fresh eggs and bacon sizzling on one of the large hot-plates. The cook waves at me and points at the food with an equally warm smile which I respond to.

Once my bag is put away, I grab a couple of slices of still warm bread, freshly baked that morning by the hired help. The prisoners do a lot of the prepping for the day's menu, as well as most of the cooking, under the watchful eye of a couple of qualified chefs. The 3 officers that work in the kitchen, just as we do in the rest of the prison, are there purely as deterrents. There are a multitude of things that can be used as weapons so it is imperative that we keep a very close eye on the proceedings. Everything from butcher's knives that are chained to tables, to slicing blades on a deli slicer. Any of the vast number of kitchen utensils the prisoners use on a daily basis are counted, checked and rechecked. Perimeter walks are conducted as well as walks along each of the tables. Its always a good reminder that, when you walk amongst the criminals, keep an eye on the length of chain on the blade they are using at the time.

My other two offsiders are already there, having started a couple of hours before. Two staff have an early start, while a third officer works a shorter shift, not only arriving later, but also finishing earlier. The rotating roster has its good points and bad points and for me, it's a definite win for the day. It makes no difference in my pay as I'm paid a salary, so being rostered on a short shift is just one of the great benefits of working here.

Sam Howell is already downing a bacon-heavy sandwich, waving a hand at me as I shovel some goodness onto my own bread. John Simons, the other officer, is gobbling a sandwich while overlooking the bakery section, four prisoners busy baking the prison's supply of bread. I walk over and shake hands, a quick chin-wag to catch up on any gossip. It's another thing that can be very active in prison.

The prison gossip train is one that is always active and always fully loaded. And it's the very thing that we love, that is responsible for it. The roster. Because people work very different shifts to everybody else, unless you are close to a particular officer and know them personally, you never know what they do or where they are. I remember a time when I went on annual leave for a month and when I returned to work, very few people realised just how long I had been away for. They simply put it down to the roster.

Once we finish our breakfast, I take over the supervision of the bakery and assume a post in one of the nearer corners. I ensure my back is close to a wall to prevent anyone from walking behind me; prevention being better than cure, if you know what I mean. If I don't give them the opportunity then I can avoid most issues. I remain at the post for a couple of hours as I watch giant mixing machines working mountains of dough which are in turn put into baking tins and placed in the industrial ovens. It's a giant production line that ends with the guy that mans the slicing machine, bagging each loaf once done.

Everyone works in silence, a few comments and jokes thrown out here and there. Each joke is met with a sudden burst of laughter which ends just as quickly. The prisoners each work their stations to ensure the line remains productive with each person having a set quota to reach. They work one of two shifts and once they reach their numbers, are allowed to leave. once they've been wanded for metal and also given a pat-down for any goods that may have found their way into pockets, they are returned to their units.

It's mid-morning by the time the first issue arises. A loud barrage of swearing suddenly erupts from the far end of the kitchen, the expletives flying thick and fast. As I go to investigate, I can already see the issue as a prisoner holds his hand close to himself, the chopping station behind him. He's managed to slice his finger and as he holds it up for me to see, blood trickles onto the concrete floor.

"Alright, hold it close," I said and reach for a roll of paper towel sitting on a bench. I hand him a large chunk of it as I hear Sam call a code Mike. Within a few minutes the staff begin to arrive, quickly followed by the nurses. They assess the wound and determine that it requires stitching and ask for the crook to be escorted to the medical wing. A couple of staff members offer to take him and we return to our previous positions, work resuming without hesitation.

When lunchtime count is called, a lot of the crooks begin to pack up their stations, their shifts ending once the count is called correct. It's effectively a changeover of the work crews and Sam and I facilitate the wanding and pat downs once we finish counting up our numbers. I grab the hand-wand and begin scanning the prisoners one at a time. It's a pretty important time as any number of metallic items could be hidden, to be used as weapons once properly fashioned into whatever weapon they had in mind. Sam is conducting pat downs and as I finish with my last one, look at the prisoner he is currently checking. I nearly burst out laughing when I see the insanely huge bulge in the front of his shorts. I tap Sam on the back and when he looks at me, point at the "discreet" package. The crook has an animated grin as he realises that he's been busted. He doesn't kick up, understanding that he's been caught and will be sacked from his position. His haul? A dozen sausages that he's managed to stuff into the front of his underpants; raw and without wrapping, the only package being his own. He hands them over and then follows us into a private room where we now conduct a full strip search. This reveals a small bag of coffee hidden in his shoe; a bag of sugar in his other shoe; half a dozen slices of bacon in one armpit, again without wrapping. As he turns and bends over, I see the end of a plastic bag protruding from his anus and he laughs as he slowly tugs on it when asked. It gradually escapes the confines of his arsehole and when we finally unbag it, discover half a dozen small balloons which later turn out to contain ICE.

For us, the ICE is a valuable find and could mean that one of the deliveries that had arrived that morning, could have been the source of contraband. The intelligence squad will use this information and track whoever had made deliveries that morning, comparing it to previous finds and deliveries. Every bit of information helps and once we phone the sup with our find, complete our reports, which we send out to everyone who needs it. The crook is not only fired from his job, but also separated into a management unit until the risk is determined. He may have been the mule and once the owners of the drugs find out he's been caught, may come calling for payback which can be thorough.

The afternoon shift arrives about half an hour later and the processes restart. Although the bakery section closes after lunchtime count, there are still plenty of stations to watch as prison meals are prepared by the hundreds. Each unit will send their respective billets up to get their unit's meal trolleys and then return them once the meals have been served.

It's a casual afternoon, highlighted by another cut finger, a code mike for someone with back pain, and one small altercation that resulted in a thrown saucepan that crashed into a wall. It's dealt with quite quickly and tempers eased.

When I walk out alone a few hours later, I'm whistling, happy to be going home. Today, has been a good day.

Wednesday, September 5

I'm back for another day in the kitchen and another short shift. There's an extra skip in my step as I walk through the door, knowing that after tomorrow's shift, I have a 3-day break. I'm off on a road trip with my wife and I can not wait to leave this place behind, even if only for a few days. Sam and John are already in as I arrive and I grab breakfast after putting my things away. I check the menu board as I chomp down on a bacon and egg sandwich and see that one of my favourite foods is being made today; donuts. The prison has a rotating menu, which means that the same food is served week in week out. Fridays is fish and chip day, for instance, and Mondays is always tuna casserole day. Wednesday's dessert is donut and, for someone with a sweet tooth, the best dessert day of all.

The prisoners are already busy preparing the batter and heating the fryers. The bakery is still in operation, Sam overseeing the area. I go and stand near the donut boys and watch as they bring the doughy mess into a beautiful reality. Trays and trays of donuts need to be prepared, with each prisoner receiving one for dessert that evening. That means hundreds of them need to be made and I'm just the man to watch over them. I stand and watch, finishing my breakfast, when there is a sudden uproar from the other side of the kitchen. Two Asian prisoners are yelling at each other in Vietnamese, their words not making any sense. But sometimes language isn't really needed when you can see the issue as plain as day. One has not kept up with demand and the other is telling him to pull his finger out of his arse. The quicker they fill their quota, the quicker they finish and this one clearly wasn't too fussed with his speed level. Sam goes over to them and settles them down as John walks over as back-up. The situation is quietened down almost immediately, neither prisoner wanting things to escalate. Sometimes the best thing for an officer to do is just make their presence known. It's not about running in and waving your arms about. If it can be taken care of now, on their terms, then the chances of repercussions later on in the unit can be dramatically reduced. And that's a win for everybody.

All the donuts are finished and packed by 2 that afternoon and when the last of the trays has been put on the trolley and wheeled into the cool room, the moment of glory arrives. One of the cooks, carrying glory before him, sets a loaded tray of hot jam donuts on one of the benches, waving one arm back and forth across the dish like a game-show host presenting a grand prize.

"Enjoy," he says and steps back as a rush of bodies push past him, mine included, a jumble of eager hands reaching for the sweet-smelling reward. There's enough for everyone to eat their fill; five hot jam donuts finding their way into my belly. It's the highlight of an otherwise simple and quiet day. Some days are just not filled with the stuff that fills pages and sells books, but for us, those are the days we appreciate the most.

As I walk out a couple of hours later, the sweet taste of jam still lingering on my lips, I find out that I'm back in the medical wing in the morning. I drop by to see how it is going in there on my way past and am pleased to hear that it has also been a pretty quiet day in there as well. Hopefully, tomorrow will be the same. Today has been a very good day.

Thursday, September 6

When I return to the medical wing the next day, I'm greeted by that all too familiar hint of shit that I know will never disappear after that horrible day the previous month. It's like its permanently entrenched into the floors. Vicky Temple and Scott Jones are already in the unit and we greet each other with handshakes all round. Behind us, in their own little area, 2 nurses are having a heated debate and, by the sounds of it, are not likely to agree anytime soon. It's unclear to us what it's about and, as long as they don't start to tangle each other physically, we don't get involved.

The morning muster is finished within a few minutes and once count is called correct; I unlock the first lot of prisoners from their hospital cells. They begin to shuffle out; half out into the courtyard to catch some early spring rays, the other half pacing up and down the corridors. A couple flick the TV on whilst another one jumps on the treadmill. I return to the station and check the day's moves, looking for any names that are currently residing in here. There are no names that match and I close the list down and engage a prisoner in conversation. He's standing close by and he asks about one of my tattoos. It's a black circle surrounding something that resembles a strange letter K; it's the symbol for "Ka" from the Dark Tower series, by Stephen King.

"Is that like a peace symbol?" he asks, pointing a finger at my forearm. He's a fairly new prisoner, aged in his late 30's.

"No," I said, shaking my head. "Do you read, William?" I ask and he ponders for a bit.

"Sometimes, not much though."

"It's a symbol from a book by my favourite author. Ever read any Stephen King?" He shakes his head.

"Watched the Shining once. Scared the shit out of me," he said, laughing a little. We talk for a bit and he listens while I explain the meaning of the symbol. I always appreciate talking to prisoners when they are interested in what I have to say. He asks me more about the story of the Dark Tower and I give him a brief rundown of the 8-book odyssey. It's one of my favourite subjects and one that I enjoy talking about. It's rare that I meet people interested in

Stephen King and when I do, I try and help them understand the amazing breadth of his work, often misunderstood as being just horror.

It's a good hour before William returns to his cell and I begin locking the prisoners up shortly after. It's time for the next group to come out for their time out in the open and the changeover is quick and efficient. The new group almost mimics the first, some going outside while others congregate around the TV and treadmill. The whole process repeats itself a couple more times throughout the day, each change over running smoothly and quickly. There are some places within this prison that are just meant to be laid back and this is one of them.

Having a couple of easy days in a row is somewhat of a blessing as I know that it won't last forever. It never does in this place and although I know there's drama in the future, I try and enjoy the peace while I have it. It's an enjoyable day and when I walk out a few hours later, look forward to my upcoming road trip.

Today was a great day.

Friday, September 7

Rostered day off.

Saturday, September 8

Rostered day off.

Sunday, September 9

Rostered day off.

Monday, September 10

It's quite hard to walk back into the prison after an amazing weekend away. But as we all know, no matter how long the holiday, they always come to an end and reality resumes all too quickly. I head to Thomson east, a main stream unit housing a variety of prisoners including one significant group from a motorcycle gang. I won't name them but as is common knowledge, there are a large number of outlaw motorcycle clubs and when thrown together in a room, don't tend to play well together.

The unit is quiet as I enter and I immediately pack my things away. I head to the officer's station and as I sit, hear the door open as 2 other officers enter the unit. A massive smile begins to grow on my face as I see a familiar face walk in. It's my friend Kon Giopoulos, an officer that almost died in the prison a couple of months ago (see June edition). Today is Kon's first day back and I exit the station to greet him. We hug it out and he tells me that he's glad to be back. It's been a long road to full recovery but he's been given the all clear and here he is.

Normally, officers are put on light duties upon returning from an injury. Kon is not one to take on any form of light duties. He's a very proud man and working units is what he does. The other officer, Thelma Wallace, is also a veteran of the place. I'm in very good company and look forward to the day. As we enter the station, a sudden commotion erupts in a cell on the upper deck, almost above us. We can hear the crooks yelling at each other, accompanied by the flat cracks of slaps and punches. Thelma follows me as I head upstairs, go to the cell door and drop the trap. I look in and can see two prisoners appearing to cuddle each other, blood dripping from one of their mouths. I kick the door a couple of times and get their attention. They immediately release each other and head to opposite ends of the cell.

"Guys, what's going on?" I ask.

"Caught this fucking rat stealing my chips," one of them yells, pointing at the other prisoner. Thieving, as contradictory as it sounds, is a definite no-no and for the prisoner accused of the crime, will almost certainly mean a unit move. Not only will the commotion have been heard by adjoining cells, but the crook who accused him will almost certainly tell his mates. The one accused, looks to be no older than 20, small and meek. His name is Bobby Thomas and he's only been in prison for a couple of days. He hangs his head in shame, the bag of chips in question, lying crushed on the floor between them.

Thelma heads back down the stairs and phones the Sup. Once she has clearance, she returns and between us, we unlock the cell to remove the thief for his own protection. Kon is already on the phone to the Vacancy department and after informing them of the details, is given a new unit for the crook. He's off to a protection unit and once count is called correct, will be moved before the unit is unlocked. I hope for his sake; he learns to keep his fingers to himself. He's likely to have them cut off in here, if he doesn't learn quickly.

We finish our count and, once Control calls count correct, arrange with Loddon South to send their transport officer to come and get this kid. Kon and I head back to his cell and take the other one out so the kid can pack his things up. We give the other one a chance to put his things up on his bunk to ensure nothing else is stolen. Kon and I stand watch as the kid packs and, once he's done, hand him over to the transport officer. He exits the unit to a chorus of dog-whistles and cheers.

Once they are safely out, Kon and I begin to unlock the unit, prisoners exiting their cells and heading to their respective activities. Some head to the toasters for breakfast while others head to the laundry and begin their washing. A few head to the officer's station and others begin using the gym equipment. There's no gymnasium today so the prisoners will keep busy on the unit equipment, which in itself, is quite adequate.

Thelma is standing in the station and is already inundated with questions by the time Kon and I return. As we begin to facilitate requests, the morning medication trolley enters and a lot of the prisoners begin to form a line in front of the dispensary window. The line is quiet and for once, everyone seems to just want to get their meds and get on with their day. There's only one little flare up when one of the newer prisoners tries to get his medication without his ID card. But when the rest of the crooks begin burning him, he quickly retreats and goes back to his cell to get his card. When he re-joins the back of the line, he stands quietly, his head staring at the floor.

Once the med trolley exits after the last of the meds are given, the unit settles into it's usual routine. 2 prisoners are transferred out to other units and 1 transfers in. There are a couple of cell re-shuffles and most of the work is completed by the time lunchtime count is called correct a few hours later.

The afternoon goes by as we watch several prisoners play cards; a table-tennis match; several prisoners play pool as well as the usual line-up of fitness exercises. It's around 2 o'clock when Kon and I agree to conduct our random cell searches. We are pleased when 2 of the 3 cells allocated for searching prove to be vacant and when we approach the third, see that it's occupied by a quiet Asian, named Tran. He is about as straight as they come; in jail for drug smuggling.

Many Vietnamese are in our jail and for 99% of them, it's due to drug smuggling. After we strip Tran and search his person, we let him leave and we search as best we can. The cell is so clean that we struggle to fault anything. Every bit of surface is clean and free from dirt and dust and there is nothing out of place. After searching fruitlessly for almost 20 minutes, we exit the cell and return to the station.

The games continue and for us at least, it's another afternoon that we can take it easy. The prisoners behave themselves for the rest of the day and as we exit the prison as a group a couple of hours later, I'm glad to see my mate back at work. It's been a long time without him but I can see that he's happy to be back where he belongs.

Today was a good day.

Tuesday, September 11

Woke up feeling very ordinary and decide to utilize a sick day. I remain in bed for the rest of the day and enjoy a 3-day break.

Wednesday, September 12

Rostered day off.

Thursday, September 13

Rostered day off.

Friday, September 14

The Sally port is not one of those places that people will actively volunteer for, yet for me, it still remains one of the few places where I feel like I'm not part of the prison. For one thing, there is absolutely no prisoner contact, unless of course, the Day Sup escorts one out for his discharge. It is also a place where you have very little staff contact, the only "faces" from the prison being shadow shapes behind reflective glass that watch you from the control room. Other than that, it's basically trucks and buses and the drivers of each that you deal with.

Today was a day where I literally felt at home. And I only had today to go before I was going away for a few days to drive interstate. My wife and I were heading up the coast to visit her Dad for a few days. He'd been doing it tough after falling quite ill and we decided to both take some annual leave and head up to see him for a few days.

 The morning rush of court buses coming in and out of the prison was well and truly under way by the time I arrived for my shift a little after 5. The night officer, some new officer I'd never met before, waved at me and then disappeared almost as quick. Some people just weren't born with the basic courtesies of life. But I wasn't too fussed; instead, I was happy to be there.

Once I put my things away, I waited for control to raise or lower the roller doors at either end of the area. I could see movement through tiny little slits in the metallic roller shutters and heard the voices of people from both sides. The inner door made a sudden crumple of disapproval and a second later began to retract; slowly winding itself up and up and up. It revealed a bus carrying prisoners to court. Once the roller door had reached its pinnacle, the bus slowly rolled forward, creeping over several CCTV cameras that were embedded in the floor. I watched the monitor as it drove over the cameras and then, once I was satisfied it was all clear, gave the thumbs up for control to bring the roller shutter down again. Only when it is secured does the driver and offsider exit their vehicle.

"Morning Simon, we have 5" the passenger calls out to me. I wave back, flashing a smile at her. They both approach and I enter the cabin of their truck, ensuring they have no hidden passengers or contraband inside. I also confirm that they are carrying their phones and iPad. The book marks their incoming belongings and this need to be married up on exit. Anything left behind is considered smuggled contraband and can carry charges as well as instant dismissal. It's definitely not the way you'd want to lose your job.

Once their cabin checks out, I do a quick walk around of their vehicle and check that all the doors are secured and latched. An unlocked door is considered a major security breach and again, carries very harsh penalties. The bus checks out and another thumbs up to control begins to raise the outer roller shutter. It slowly trundles up its tracks as the two officers return to their cabin. I turn to the control window and hold up 5 fingers to signify the number of prisoners onboard. Once the door is fully raised, they start the bus and slowly drive out. Another bus is already waiting outside the door and the drivers wave at each other as they pass and the incoming bus enters the sally port. It too drives over the cameras embedded in the floor and the process is repeated. Incoming buses are processed a little different though.

As the door trundles shut again, the officers exit their vehicle and are themselves searched for any contraband. They are wanded with a hand-held metal detector and remove their boots for inspection. I check the cabin and also ensure the doors are secured. Once I'm satisfied that the bus is clear, I give control a thumbs up as well as signalling a closed fist to them. This means that the bus is empty and is carrying a count of zero prisoners. As the control room keeps a tally of the prison count, it is imperative that they maintain a clear understanding of how many prisoners are coming in and out of the prison; a count that is directly dependant on me.

There are about a dozen morning trucks for me to check during entry to the prison, and then recheck during their exit. It's a process that I will repeat multiple times throughout the day and one that one gets very familiar with as the day wears on. As well as court buses, there are delivery trucks that need to be thoroughly searched. Delivery trucks can be seen as one avenue of introducing contraband, such as any type of modern technology, drugs, alcohol and tobacco. It's probably fair to say that multiple movies and TV shows have gotten this part right. Unfortunately for us, smuggling small things in can be very simple as we are limited with what we can actually search. Anything sealed, such as food containers, is out of bounds as these items have been factory sealed at another location. And yet every day, things will make their way in and be freely distributed right under our noses.

The other thing that happens in the Sally port, and as read about with rather comical results (see August edition) are when prisoners are discharged from prison; when they have completed their sentences or are granted parole. This can result in various different experiences, from the good as you watch joy and relief on a first-timer who might actually use the prison experience as a genuine lesson and never return; to the ones that like to flip you the bird as they tell you to "keep the fucken bed warm, Dog". But in the end, it really makes no difference. Stay out, come back, it doesn't matter one way or the other.

There are quite long stretches of time between buses and trucks at times and it's these times where, if you have some, can catch up on other things; be it reading a book or magazine, drawing or writing. I think you can guess what I do during those times, the results of which you are reading right now.

There are a few codes throughout the day, mainly code mikes called for unwell prisoners that require medical attention in their respective units. There is one code foxtrot but I don't find out the details due to my isolated position. For me, it's actually a good thing as I use it as a break from the shit; for you, I guess, not so much.

If you think that there's action on a daily basis, at every site in the prison, then I'm sorry to say there's not. Very little "drama" happens in the Sally port. It's just a day of processing and searching; of idle chit-chat and minor introductions to new drivers. But for me, it also serves as a tiny break from the stresses and awareness of what the rest of the prison still endures.

For me, the day is a good one.

Saturday, September 15

Annual leave

Sunday, September 16

Annual leave

Monday, September 17

Annual leave

Tuesday, September 18

Annual leave

Wednesday, September 19

Annual leave

Thursday, September 20

My first night shift in quite some time and my heart sinks down into my feet as I realise that I'm in Murray South for the night. Of all the management units, this one was the absolute worst. Comprised of 3 separate areas in the one building, the station is placed in such a position that all the cells, except the ones located in solitary, can see everything you do, thanks to some ventilation mesh that's embedded into each cell door. You are watched by close to 60 sets of eyes from the moment you enter the unit and, if the prisoners are in the right frame of mind, can burn you for hours.

The day-staff greet me as I enter the unit, all happy to be within minutes of the end of their shift. Jason Parker takes me through the highlights of the day and also shows me the 2 watches I have. Both are S2's, meaning half-hourly observations throughout the night. The other 4 staff commence their lock-down counts as I stow my things away. It doesn't take long for control to call the count correct and within mere minutes of showing up, I'm left alone.

From the way the crooks begin yelling, I know that it's going to be a long night. They either burn one of their own or burn the night officer; it's usually one or the other and if the night officer isn't a regular face that they know, that's who cops it. I can tell you from experience, it's not easy. The abuse is raw, nasty and very, very personal. They yell everything from raping your mother, wife or sister, to hot-watering you when you give them their breakfast in the morning. If you ever find yourself in this situation, the best advice I can give you is to ignore it. I know it's not easy to do, believe me, I really do. The irony is that I'm actually sitting in the very same unit, during a night shift, as I'm writing this passage for you about the night in question (and yes, I'm writing this while being burnt). It is just baiting, the crooks hoping that they get a reaction because, if they do, they know they have you. Do not give in.

"Aye dog, shoulda brought your mother with ya," one yells.

"Were your parents related, ya fuckin mutt?" yells another. I can turn a television on if I choose, but I'd rather spend my spare time writing. It allows me to focus on other things while riding the abuse. If I cave, the abuse will never end. And so, the night begins with me checking my emails, while keeping an eye on the CCTV monitors of the main areas. I can also hear abuse from the solitary area and can hear them burning some poor fool in there. The target was transferred into the unit just a few hours prior and it isn't long before he caves.

It's less than an hour into my shift and the intercom buzzes. When I answer it, a quiet voice slowly creeps out to me.

"Boss," he whispers.

"Yes, what's up?" I ask.

"I can't guarantee my own safety," he said and I groan inside. It's not a genuine cry for help or threat of suicide; it's a bail. He just wants to get out because of the burning. I know this because he is whispering to me. The reason he's whispering is because he doesn't want anyone to hear his call for help. If they catch wind of his attempted bail, the burning will increase ten-fold.

Even though I know it's nothing more than an attempted bail, it isn't my call to judge. I have neither the qualification to make that assumption, nor the authority. As far as I'm concerned, the threat is as real as any other.

"Sit tight and I'll get someone to come and chat with you. You'll be OK for a few minutes, yeah?" I ask and he says he'll wait. Of course, he will. It takes me a few minutes to ascertain the night psych's whereabouts, but when I do, request their attendance.

The night psych, Walleed, arrives a few minutes later and I escort him to the cell. I stand by as he attempts to talk to the crook through the trap but the other prisoners have cottoned on to what's about to happen and commence an assaultive barrage of abuse that is so loud, the nurse is unable to hear the crook's voice. Although he tries for several minutes, it's an impossible task and he eventually beckons me out into an adjoining office. He asks me for alternatives and I ask him to sit tight while I contact the night supervisor. When Clare arrives, I give her a rundown and she calls for extra staff to assist. Once we have almost half a dozen officers, we escort the crook to a room that's located in one of the other sections. He is now comfortable enough to speak with the psych and once he does, admits that he just wants to get out of the unit. Clare tells him that the prison is full and it will be impossible to remove him now; he'd have to wait until the morning. But he shakes his head, determination in his eyes telling us that he'd rather do something stupid than return to his cell.

The psych beckons us out of the room and the crook is left sitting at the table, his hands cuffed in front of him. There's only a table with attached seats so he's unable to use anything against us. The nurse begins to explain the situation to us and as we listen, I see the crook stand, walk near a wall and begin slamming his head into it; low flat thuds emanating out to us with each impact.

"It's not gonna change anything," the nurse says through the door and the prisoner stops and sits back down. He knows how to play the game and that's exactly how I've come to see it; nothing more than a silly game of chicken. Prisoners know how to manipulate the system to their needs and this is one of those ways.

"Just escort him to the medical unit," Clare says. "We'll have to move someone out of one of the observation cells and into another unit for the night." And just like that, the crook wins the game and is escorted out. As he exits the room, the unit erupts into a crescendo of abuse and dog whistles as the other prisoners let their feelings known. The crook keeps his head low as he's led out and, just like that, it's just me and the remaining sets of eyes again.

It's another couple of hours before the unit begins to settle down, a couple of "under the door" conversations going on here and there. They leave me alone for the most part and that suits me fine. It gives me the headspace to do some writing. It's just after midnight before the unit is silent, except for the occasional cough, bed fart and flushing toilet.

The rest of the night progresses slowly as I tap away on my keyboard. Clare visits around 2 in the morning and, after a brief chat, she continues on her rounds. The day staff begin to arrive a little before 7 and after a brief handover of the previous night's events, I bid my temporary goodbyes and head out.

I hate that unit, but all things aside, I'm walking out and that means it must have been an OK night.

Friday, September 21

As much as it pains me to write this, and I mean this sincerely, I hate telling you that I returned back to Murray South for a second night. If the previous night was bad then tonight can only be described as a complete fuck up, from start to finish. I can already hear the shouting well before I enter the corridor that leads up the unit entrance, feeling like I want to rip my heart out and nail it to the fence for the night; maybe grab it back if I walk past here in the morning.

Jason is sitting in the station as I enter and I hear a couple of crooks greet me, prison style. But their greetings immediately evaporate, like water off a duck's back; Jack is grinning at me and it's the type of grin that quickly births a groan in my throat.

"Got a new arrival coming. He's about five minutes away and just in time for you," he said, the sarcasm biting me like fingers on a chalkboard. I was already wound up, not only from the previous night but also just by being back in here now.

"Oh yeah? Is it Ricky Gervais? Coming in to entertain us for the night?" I said, my own sarcasm sounding deflated and weak.

"Toby Manning," a voice from behind me says and as I turn around, see Vicky Temple enter the station. Her grin matches the one sitting before me perfectly. I hear an internal thump as my heart hits the floor and begins convulsing. What can I say about Toby Manning? (see August edition) Painful, hard work, a handful, irritating, messed up; and did I mention painful?

"Thanks, guys," I said and put my bag away, sitting down in one of the chairs and watching as two other officers begin evening count. The voices from within the cells are still enthusiastic, as they continue their conversations about lost girlfriends, stolen cars, and one on the bottom deck that was explaining to a couple of others how to break into a particular model of bus. Go figure.

When count is called correct twenty minutes later, the day crew make their way out of the unit, telling me to have a good night with sarcastic grins and little snickers. It might be a little facetious, but there's no malice intended on their behalf. All of them had been in my situation before; each having served their own night duties in here.

The phone rings almost immediately and I'm advised that a couple of Tactical officers are escorting Toby up now. I acknowledge the call and hang up. His cell is on the bottom deck and one of the closest to my station and so, I head over and unlock the door. The prisoners already know about the move; the prison telegraph transmitting faster than phone calls between officers at times.

"Toby is coming," one yells, and although there are a few laughs and howls, I can hear their own apprehension. Like I said, Toby can be very painful and, as you'll read soon, not just to officers.

The doors open a few minutes later and a grinning Toby walks in, flanked by two officers that tower over him by at least 18 inches. He's about 5'6, 32-years old, and is thin and wiry. Although he used to have hair, he's now bald, thanks to some manipulation by his case workers. You see, one of Toby's habits is to bronze up (look up the meaning in the prison terms section at the beginning of this book if you're unsure of what that means), and at times, enjoyed using his own shit as hair wax and giving himself "poohawks" as he called them.

He flashes me a grin as he walks in and shows me his now vacant gums; his teeth all removed due to decay.

"Hello Mr King," he says as he heads for his unit.

"Hey Toby," I said, recognising the grin only too well. Toby's IQ is around 30, having the mental age of an 8-year old. This makes him very susceptible to influence from the other prisoners which, I hoped, would work in my favour. They also began to greet Toby under their doors, yelling things out to him. Toby heard them and I could see his head lift a little higher, his shoulders drawing back a little as he walked proudly into his cell like a regular idol. As the tactical boys follow him in, Toby turns on them and his voice instantly turns to one of hatred and threat. He holds his cuffed hands out to the officers, beckoning them to uncuff him.

"Take these off, you fucken maggot," he said to them, his voice loud enough to carry out into the unit and I can see the delight on his face when the prisoners begin to cheer him, egging him on for more. As he sees me standing outside the door, he grins again. "What are you looking at, dog? Fuckin dog." The unit erupts into gales of laughter as the officers remove the shackles and exit his cell. As they close his door, I hear him spit at them, but the door slams home before it hits anybody.

"Fuckin dogs," comes from within the cell as Toby begins to kick the door, the loud booms exploding in my ears. They are so loud that you think your brain is rattling.

"Leave him with you," the officers say to me, the same shit-eating grin on their faces as were on the day staff before them. I thank them in my own sarcastic fashion and see them out, once again, alone with my crooks.

The banging and shouts from Toby continue for a while, and pretty soon the other prisoners grow tired of it. It makes it not only hard to hold conversations, but the banging is loud enough to make watching television almost impossible. I can hear a couple of the prisoners telling Toby to stop but it's like trying to talk to a rabid dog. I dial in his intercom and try and get his attention. For a moment I only hear him kicking and panting, still yelling the same abuse at the now-gone officers that walked him up. He thinks he's impressing the other prisoners, but unbeknownst to him, they are starting to get pretty pissed with him. When he finally hears me on the intercom, he stops the kicking and I hear him walk over to the speaker.

"What do you want, Dog," he shouts, still trying to play to his audience. I try and calm him down, asking him how his day was, but he doesn't listen, resuming his abuse. It's no good and I hang up. He presses the intercom and starts shouting as soon as I answer. I hang up again and he presses the button again, and again, and again. I have no choice but to answer the call as the intercoms are not only seen as an emergency device but are also 100% monitored by a government department. I begin to hear more prisoners call on Toby to shut up and once he hears the calls, finally begins to quieten. I hang up the intercom but he immediately re-calls. I call the Night Sup and explain the situation. He gives me the OK to leave the intercom open with the volume turned down until he's asleep. Calls from other cells can still be received, but Toby's connection needs to be broken before they can be answered. As a new call notification comes in, I hang up on Toby and answer the next call in line. They are simple calls such as handing out toilet paper, requests for food which are denied, and the ever-present request for coffee; again denied.

Once they finally give up trying to get me to hand shit out, I leave the connection to Toby open and finally check my emails. It's nearly 10 o'clock and it feels good to have the unit quiet. Conversations are still progressing around the place but, for the most part, they leave me alone. Just as I'm about to close the email program, I hear a faint sound that I recognize immediately. I turn the intercom up a bit and listen.

"Gonna flood up, Cunt," I hear Toby say, the familiar rush of a shower in the background. It's a game he knows only too well and one that I have been known to play a few times; crooks like him on one side, and officers with no choice on the other. I go to the water cabinet that's next to his cell and, once I open it up, begin to turn the taps off that supply water to his cell. I know what will come next and, although I'd rather keep the shower running, it's something that I must do. I hear the water begin to slow, then quit completely, Toby kicking the door a couple of times in disgust. "Think that's gonna work, Dog?" he yells and I return to the station, ready for round 2.

It's almost midnight by the time the unit is finally completely quiet, the only sounds being the low TV sounds emanating from various cells. The prison has (I know, I know) a special movie channel that plays latest-release movies 24-hours a day and some prisoners, especially those that are confined to their cells for 23 of those 24 hours, prefer to watch TV by night and sleep by day. I turn my own TV on and begin flicking through the channels. I come across a Gordon Ramsay thing and begin to watch. What can I say; he's the only one on TV that speaks my kind of language. I watch as he goes into some idiot's cool room and discovers boxes of rotten produce and mangy chicken. I try and sit a little closer to hear and then the intercom pipes up. It's Toby again and I answer him, expecting the worst.

"What's up, Toby?" I ask.

"I need some toilet paper, please."

"OK, I'll bring you some." I grab a roll from one of the cupboards and walk to his cell door. I raise the viewing window first, to make sure he isn't standing there with a cup of piss or something. I shine my torch in and see Toby standing just inside the door, his grin wide and full. At first, the dark patches on his face don't register with me and I'm about to open the trap to hand him the roll. Fireworks suddenly explode in my mind as I take a second look and shine my torch directly into his face. His face, head and shirtless torso are covered in thick, brown shit, the little bits of corn he must have eaten the previous day, smeared here and there. The smell hits me then, even through a couple of inches of steel.

"How do you like that, Dog?" he yells and begins kicking the door again. Bang, bang, bang. A couple of other crooks begin to shout for him to shut the fuck up but he doesn't stop. I return to the station and call the Sup. It's not really asking for help, just more to let them know what's going on, just in case things kick off. As I hang up, other crooks begin banging their own doors, shouts now telling Toby to pull his head in. It takes another hour to quieten things down enough for me to be able to hear him on the intercom. He still isn't talking sensibly and I have no choice but to leave the line open and once again reduce the volume. It's almost 3 by the time I hear nothing else from him. The soft snores that come through the speaker, tell me that he's finally given up.

By 6 that morning, Toby has awoken and apologized for his behaviour. He knows that his case workers will be told of his behaviour and, just like an 8-year old, wants to make good before they find out. I turn his water back on and he agrees to shower the shit off himself and clean up his cell. When I serve breakfast shortly after, his clean smile greets me and I hand him his toast. Day staff begin to arrive and I clap each on the back and tell them to enjoy. As I grab my things, I make my farewells and walk out without looking back.

Another shift in that shithole finished and I couldn't be happier as I walk out. It is after all, my weekend.

Saturday, September 22

Rostered day off.

Sunday, September 23

Rostered day off.

Monday, September 24

Rostered day off.

Tuesday, September 25

Today I was in Visits and although I was in a very good mood when I came into the prison, it didn't last long. I'm OK working with people who don't understand the finer points of being in close proximity with people who have a propensity to deal with situations that don't go the way they think they ought to, with violence and abuse. You know; people who know what can set a prisoner off and try and avoid those things in order to maintain a relatively safe environment. What I'm not OK with, is working with people that will go out of their way to stir shit up; to wind a prisoner up and look for a reaction. What those people are known as, are arsonists. The reason being, that if you work with them, you'd better carry a fire extinguisher in your back pocket so that you can put out all the little spot fires as you follow them.

If you have been following my writings, then you're probably expecting me to write one name in particular; Tony Malone. He can be, as we know, quite painful. But no, the name is not Tony Malone who, in this case, I probably would have preferred with me today. The name of the thorn that was in my side today is Brock Livingston. He'd only graduated from his induction course a couple of weeks prior and although fresh into the prison, apparently had six years' experience at another facility. I'm not one to doubt, but to be honest, didn't believe it.

As I entered the building, Robert Hall, a 45-year veteran, greeted me as he went about setting up the book. A new officer followed close behind me and when I introduced myself, he told me his name was Brock.

"Pleased to meet you," I said, offering him my hand. Robert and Brock also shook and we stowed our bags in the staff room. Once our bags and lunches were put away, we headed back into the strip area. We agreed that Robert would run the book until lunchtime and then I would take it over. I didn't mind running the book as it broke up the day a bit. And staring at naked men for 6 hours was much better than staring at them for 12.

"Why do I have to strip the whole day?" Brock asked.

"Because you're the junior today," Robert said, looking at Brock over the rim of his reading glasses. You could see by his expression that he didn't like the answer but unfortunately that's the rules. New officers get to practice their stripping skills while still settling into the job. Robert wasn't always as accommodating as me and would often throw new officers in at the deep end. It was his way of seeing whether they would sink or swim. This was after all, maximum security. It wasn't a place where you needed to be led around by the hand, being shown the ins and outs of everything that went on. Some things you just had to figure out yourself. The thing about stripping is that it brought you into close proximity with prisoners when they are at one of their most vulnerable. That meant you quickly learnt how to interact with them, whether they were in a good frame of mind or bad. Robert had heard that Brock came directly from a youth justice centre. This was a very different environment compared to 16 to 21-year old inmates.

Robert Hall had been a correctional officer for most of his life. Currently 68 years old, he started his career in maximum security back in 1973, a couple of years after I was born. He's a lovely man with a great sense of humour. He could be hard when he needed to be, but generally, was the kind of officer that didn't have anything to prove. He'd pretty much seen it all and the crooks had a certain respect for him. He was nearing retirement age and he'd told me a few times while working with him, that he didn't look forward to ending his career. His wife, Eileen, had passed away a few years ago and, with no family around, didn't really want to "sit around home alone" as he put it. The problem was, Robert was beginning to slow down considerably and he had troubling hearing. Some of the newer prisoners were giving him a hard time when he didn't hear what they were saying, especially when he asked them to repeat themselves.

Control signals a correct muster and Robert calls the front to see which visitors had arrived. Once he receives the list, he begins notifying units of which prisoners are required to attend. It's one of the few times where prisoners don't need to be asked twice about attending somewhere. Visits, the gymnasium and methadone are probably the only times that prisoners will skip out of a unit, anxious to get to their destination.

Whilst waiting for the prisoners to turn up, the phone rings and we watch as Robert answers the call, his face growing blank and grey. Brock watches him, then leans in to me to ask what the issue was. I didn't need to wait for Robert's explanation. I knew what the call was about and it was one of those things you try to avoid.

Robert hangs the phone up and checks his list. He runs his pen down and when he reaches the intended target, taps it repeatedly.

"Watson, box visit." Brock looks at him, confused. "His missus scanned positive for meth," Robert continues.

"When a visitor scans positive to drugs, and if they can't find any during the subsequent strip search, the visit can continue but has to be converted to a box visit," I tell Brock. His face lights up with recognition as he begins to understand. I watch him as I see his mind begin to tick over. Finally, after almost a full minute, he finally comprehends the consequence to changing the visit from a contact visit to a non-contact visit.

"Holy shit, he's gonna be pissed, ain't he?" he finally asks.

"Yes, he is," Robert says and looks at Brock sternly. "Maybe let me tell him and you stand back." Brock looked at him for a moment, considering his options. He took a step back and lent against the wall.

"I could do it. I'm not stupid," he mumbles but we ignore him. It's not a situation we want or need and deciding on who will tell the prisoner that he might not be able to hold his child or girlfriend or mother is not something worth debating over. Robert and I both know that the best way to deal with the situation is to simply deal with it head on and not try and sugar coat it. If we don't make a big deal of it, chances are, neither will the crook. I'm about to share this with Brock, but the door opens and four prisoners walk in.

"Boss," the first one says, greeting Robert and dropping his ID card on the table in front of him.

"Morning, boys," Robert replies and ticks each of their names off. The box visit isn't among them and I signal the first prisoner to follow me into the strip room. We go through the usual process and, as we finish, I see Brock stripping another prisoner in the adjoining room. I motion to another prisoner when the door opens and two more enter our area. I follow the crook into the strip room and just as we begin the dance, I hear Robert speak the words that are dreaded in this particular area.

"Sorry son, it's changed to a box visit."

"What? But why Boss?" the prisoner asks, his voice already frantic.

"I don't know, but your visitor will be able to shed light on it. They don't tell us what happens out the front."

"But Boss, I haven't seen my missus in weeks. Please, not a box visit." His voice is starting to crack but, looking over my shoulder, I can tell he won't go much further. His shoulders are slumped, his head down, almost defeated. If he was going to become aggressive, he would be up on his toes, his shoulders high and arms ready to strike. Aggressive prisoners don't tend to stand still and look like they need to be seated. They are up, loud, maintain eye contact and almost bounce on the spot, ready to strike. Recognizing body language is an important part of the job and as I have said in previous chapters, an officer's biggest weapon is his mouth. But, as in many examples of sheer stupidity, it can also be the greatest betrayer; especially on an inexperienced officer with a bad case of attitude.

"Dude, wanna shut the fuck up? Get in here so I can strip ya," were the words that I heard next. Not from Robert but from Brock. He had the intelligence level of a door handle and I'm pretty sure you know what happened next. Watson turned and within a split second was in Brock's face.

"You shut the fuck up, screw dog," he screamed, spittle flying from his lips. Brock's face turned crimson as I saw him look at me, his fingers starting to fumble for his radio. "Rip your fuckin tongue outa your head, cunt." He kept his hands down by his side and I saw Brock begin to raise his own, defensively. I saw another crook turn and take a step towards the two men.

"Sit down, Jason," I said to him and he looked at me with apprehension. "Brock, let it go," I said, turning back to the two. Robert sat in his chair, completely surprised at the stupidity of the newer officer. But Watson was fired up and I could see he was about to explode. And then, as if still in doubt about the volatility of the prisoner, Brock made the second mistake of the morning. Rather than use a clearance strike to keep the prisoner back, Brock grabbed Watson around the throat with one hand and tried to pull him forward. He actually wanted to go toe to toe with a crook that had been actively pumping weights for four years straight.

I was left with no choice but to hit the duress button on my radio and call a code alpha as Watson grabbed Brock by the shirt and half picked him up, smashing him back into the wall behind them. Robert yelled for the other prisoners to get into one of the strip rooms and locked them in, preventing them from joining the scuffle. I yelled at Watson to step back and let Brock go but he wasn't listening. Instead, he reached up and grabbed Brock's throat with both hands, his hands as strong as vices. With little choice, I brought my fist down on Watson's forearm as hard as I could and broke his hold on Brock. He turned on me in a split second and took a step towards me, his fists at the ready. I instinctively performed a clearance strike as he took yet another step towards me, deflecting him to my side. All it would have taken then was for someone to give him a slight push and Watson would have stumbled into an open strip room where he could have been locked up until he either cooled down or the Tactical Officers removed him. Either way, it would have been a closed case with a simple report.

If only things had of happened like that. But like I said, inexperience can be traitorous in this place. Before I could react, what happened next played out in an almost slow-motion movie; a movie I was helpless to stop. I watched as Brock was rubbing his throat; the look on his face more embarrassment than anger. He was looking at the floor and appeared to be calm. Watson was trying to regain his balance, rubbing his forearm. Robert was standing opposite to me, shaking his head. I heard the door open as officers were getting ready to assist. Then, without the slightest warning and moving so fast, Brock took two steps forward, pushed me aside and wound his fist back. He pistoned his punch straight out, connecting with the back of Watson's head. His push had knocked me off balance as I stumbled backwards and I saw Robert lunge forward much too slowly, unable to stop the attack.

I saw Watson's eyes flicker, roll upwards, then close before he hit the floor as officers piled into the room, some grabbing Brock and dragging him back. I saw a look of bewilderment in Robert's face as one of the other people called a code mike.

The commotion that followed can only be described as shocking. The strip rooms had a small side window down the side of each door. The crooks that had been locked away watched the whole mess unfold and were going ballistic in their room. One of them had punched the window, smashing it and opening up three fingers on his hand with blood pouring down the white door. All three were screaming and the room was echoing so bad, my head felt like it was rattling from the noise. I looked down and saw Watson shaking uncontrollably, the seizure gripping him tightly. He'd hit his head on the floor when he fell and blood was pooling to the side of his face.

It took a good twenty minutes for everything to be brought back under control. The nurses arrived within minutes and were treating Watson, who had stopped seizing by then. Several tactical officers brought the 3 crooks in the strip room under control and the one with an injured hand was off having it fixed. Brock was taken up the front where he would be required to complete an officer's report. Robert and I were also now filling out our reports while everything was still fresh in our minds. The prison remained operational but the Visits centre had been closed for the time being as we tended to our reports.

"I should have stopped him," Robert suddenly said as we sat, breaking the silence, the clicking of the keyboards suddenly stopping.

"It wasn't your fault, Rob," I replied. "You handled it exactly the way it should have been. Brock fucked up." But Robert shook his head.

"No, I should have known he'd act that way. I knew Watson would kick off. I should have handled it better. And I could have stopped his punch. I was right there." He paused, wiped his eyes and looked at the ceiling. Then he looked at his hands as he held them in front of his face. "Too dam slow these days. Maybe my prison days are over."

"Rob, you're fine. You're an amazing officer. No-one could have stopped Brock except Brock. Don't beat yourself up over it. Seriously." He nodded and after a moment resumed typing, his fingers slowly clicking the keys as they danced across the keyboard. I looked at him a second longer, his face looking tired and weary.

The visits centre was reopened just after lunch time muster was called correct and we received a replacement officer, Tom Grady, to fill in for Brock. The Supervisor had dropped in to check on our reports and told us that Brock had been suspended pending an investigation. He said that it didn't take long for them to make the decision based on the security-camera footage.

A lot of visitors had decided to go home by the time visits resumed and as such, our afternoon passed with very little fanfare. There was another code alpha in Tambo East which turned out to be a disgruntled crook who was looking forward to a visit from his brother. The brother turned out to be the "not hangin' around' kind of guy and as such, missed the visit. The prisoner was taken to one of the management units and prison life continued.

Robert is very quiet as we walk out a few hours later. His head is low and he looks as though his thoughts weigh heavy on his shoulders.

"You OK, Rob?" I asked as we walk. He looks at me and shrugs his shoulders.

"Everything has to end sometime, I guess," he said in a low voice.

"You're a great officer, Robert. You can't beat yourself up over someone else's fuck up. I'll see you tomorrow, yeah?" I said and held out my hand. He took it and shook, smiling at me.

"Thanks, Simon."

I run into the Sup out in the carpark and he tells me that Brock is looking at a pretty straight forward charge of assault. The video footage did not look good and he would be a very lucky man if he got off. I can share the outcome with you now as I'm writing this a couple of months later.

Brock was sacked from the prison a couple of days later and it was Watson that asked for him not to be charged. He said he brought it on himself and Brock was only defending himself. To me, Brock took a cheap shot and punched a prisoner in the back of the head. There is no justification in attacking a prisoner when he has his back turned unless that prisoner is attacking another officer. He could have been pushed into the strip room but Brock punched him square in the back of the head.

I have my own opinion on this matter and one that I won't share. It is up to each person to make their own mind up about what they consider to be appropriate force used in that type of situation. And I'll let you decide whether Brock should have been charged or not. But even in prison, no-one is above the law, whether in an officer's uniform or a prisoner's.

Wednesday, September 26

Today, I worked in Admissions and although it is normally an awesome place to work, sometimes it can also be quite volatile. Tempers can flare as prisoners go through the processes of being admitted into the prison. As soon as I enter the building, I make my way to the book to check out the list of movements for the day. Depending on the number of transfers, the list alone will determine whether we have a busy day or a slack one.

I greet Jack, the officer in charge of the book today and he returns the greeting with a wave, handing me the list.

"It's an OK morning but the afternoon is pretty ordinary," he says without much enthusiasm. I scan the list and see about two dozen prisoners who are headed to court as well as half a dozen that are transferring out. But at the bottom of the page, where the incoming names were listed, were close to 30 names. Jack was right; the afternoon would be a busy one once the 30 arrived.

The courts are processed first, each one picked up by staff as they are processed well before the prison is unlocked. Admissions is the only area that operates at this time due to the courts and, as such, is a hive of activity. A number of officers help with bringing the prisoners to Admissions while several more conduct strip searches. Others help with loading buses, as each bus is headed to a different court. Courts are spread all over the city and require several buses to deliver prisoners due to time constraints.

I'm asked to help with loading buses, a job I happily help with. I had seen enough penises the last few years and was pretty sure I would see more as the day went on. Besides, "loading buses" meant simply standing out in the compound as the bus staff did the actual loading. We were there as deterrents and in case anything kicked off during the loading process. It wasn't an overly difficult job and within an hour, all the buses were loaded and headed out the gate.

Because of the gap between the courts and when the outgoing transfers arrived, there was plenty of time for breakfast and a catch up with some of the other staff. There was a crowd of maybe a dozen officers as I enter the tea room and conversation is loud and animated. Officers always tend to speak loud and humour is the normal topic of conversation. We tend to pull the piss out of each other as it keeps spirits up. Despite working in such a miserable place, it allows us to keep a smile on our faces.

One officer in particular, Norman Raynes, or Norm for short, is probably one of the biggest pranksters I have ever met. Unafraid of embarrassing anyone, he has a tendency to pull the piss out of anyone; supervisors, managers and officers alike. This morning him and another officer, Eric, are goading a third officer; a muscle-bound fitness freak called Stan Rogers. I don't know how, but Norm always gets a laugh, regardless of how racist, sexist and demeaning his jokes are. While in most places his jokes could be seen as a form of bullying, it's different here. It's different because the people that work in this place have a much thicker skin than most, and tolerating shit is what we're paid for.

Watching Norm walk around the tea room, carrying empty buckets at a ludicrous distance from his sides is just plain funny and you can't help but laugh.

"Is this how you go shopping? Fuck the trolley, just a basket in each hand so you can show off your pecs?" He laughs so hard at his own joke and I think that's probably what most people laugh at the most; his laugh. It seriously sounds like Scooby-Do. He begins arm curling each empty bucket in an exaggerated fashion. "Just checking what I'm buying," and continues his harsh laughing. Eric grabs two more buckets, mimicking Norm. Norm looks at him and heads for him, buckets held out wide. "And when you meet another 'roid queen," he says, waddling towards Eric like a penguin, both trying to pass each other, but their arms blocking the way. "Fuckin aisles aren't wide enough," and more laughter follows. It's funny to watch and just as they begin almost dancing with each other, Tom Grady walks in to grab a coffee. He sees me and waves. Once he has his coffee, he walks over and we have a chat about the previous day's events. We agree that Brock is pretty much fucked. I tell Tom about Robert and how he kept saying he may have come to the end of his career. He shakes his head and claps me on the back.

"He's been around so long; this place will never let him go. It's in his blood. He'll be OK." I'm about to agree with him when control calls for count. We break off and conduct muster; count is called correct about 10 minutes later.

The outgoing transfers begin filing into Admissions 20 minutes later and Admissions staff begin the process of working through each prisoner's property and marking off individual items. It's one of the few times where officers can get an actual idea of hoarding and standovers. A prisoner's items are all individually listed on their property list. If they turn up with four pairs of Nike runners and only have one pair listed, then it's fair to assume they have somehow gotten hold of some extra pairs. Normally, looking at the crook can give an indication on whether they are standing over weaker prisoners or doing "special favours". One of the first prisoners to be processed is a young, skinny guy of about 25. He has long fingernails, a make-shift scarf around his neck made from prison pants and enough bags to fill a shopping trolley twice over. The bounce in his step and the way he shakes his butt from side to side is enough to tell us that the extra property that's about to be found, didn't come from any stand over. He gets most of his property from providing "lip service" to whichever unit is lucky enough to have him.

"Hi Damien," Norman says, greeting the overly happy prisoner. It takes the property officers a good 15 minutes to work their way through Damien's bags, adding new items while confiscating others. He's cheery and not upset when he loses a couple of brand-new pairs of Adidas runners. We all know that it won't take him long to make up for the loss once he arrives at his new home. He's stripped and allowed to dress in his private clothes for the trip west.

The rest of the group are processed and before long, the buses are once again being loaded. It's a relatively pain-free morning and before I know it, lunch-time muster is called. If only every day was as structured as today. It really does make the day go quick.

The start of the afternoon stretch begins with an amazingly slow couple of hours. With no one to process, we are left with nothing to do except wait for the incoming bus. At approximately 2.30 we are told that the bus has broken down and will be at least another couple of hours. It's time we have to spare as there is nothing happening other than the occasional prisoners returning from court. I grab a book and hide away in a corner of the building. It's a great couple of hours as no codes are called and the afternoon is smooth sailing.

The moment the bus turns up, shortly after 5, the commotion begins. It's understandable for the prisoners to be pissed as they've been crammed into their individual cells for almost 6 hours, pissing into urine bags and eating fruit sticks. I inform the billets to warm the meals up and then I head out to help with the unloading.

The groans are almost instant from the moment the doors are opened. Each cell houses a maximum of 4 crooks and we unload a cell at a time. They are identified, then led into a holding cell, where most make a beeline for the toilet. For some, the idea of pissing into a bag, less than 12 inches from the heads of 3 other prisoners, is beyond impossible and so the waiting can be daunting.

With two transfers cancelled, the remaining 28 prisoners are taken off and put into holding cells with very little fuss; all except one. Dane Reynolds, a new prisoner who only arrived in the system less than a month ago is volatile from the get-go. His abuse starts the minute the door is opened and he refuses to identify himself. We eventually separate him into his own holding cell and let him stew a bit. Although he still has access to a toilet and is fed a hot meal, he's informed that due to his uncooperativeness, he'll be processed last. He is led to the furthest cell from where we are working because we know exactly what will happen once we lock him in. The second the door is closed on him, he begins kicking the shit out of it, each bang booming through the halls. It's almost deafening and we know he'll continue until we process him. I can not describe just how loud the noise is, but if you compare it to a rock concert in your bathroom and imagine the beat bouncing off the tiled walls, that's how loud the sound is.

With the banging in our ears, we begin the process and create a production line. The prisoners are individually strip searched then interviewed; have their property processed one at a time and then see a nurse to ensure they don't have any immediate concerns. The time taken to finish each prisoner can take some time and is totally dependant on not only how cooperative they are, but also how much property they have. It's almost an hour before the first couple are finished and taken to their new units.

Dane is still banging his feet on the door as we reach the half way point and as all cells are monitored by CCTV, the book person can see what he's up to. As I walk past to grab another couple of prisoners, I stop and have a look at the monitor.

"How's he doing?" I ask Jack and he shakes his head.

"He's been punching the walls. See the blood spots?" he says and points to the monitor, at an area of the wall that looks like it's been drawn on. "That's not graffiti, that's this dickhead's blood." And just as I'm about to continue, I see Dane begin headbutting the same spot on the wall, the dark patch growing bigger and darker with each bang. "Oh fuck," Jack says and gets up, pushing past me and heading to Dane's cell. I follow him, my radio held at the ready to call a code. He'll need a code mike at the very least.

As we near the cell, we can hear the dull thumping from inside. Jack drops the trap and calls out to Dane.

"OI! DANE!" he yells, trying to get his attention. For a moment he doesn't get it, but then he kicks the door himself and I hear Dane yell back.

"GET ME THE FUCK OUTA HERE, DOG!" he screams. Jack suddenly pulls back as Dane spits at him through the trap, saliva and blood shooting through the small window. It isn't a good situation and Jack pulls his radio to call a code alpha. The spitting is classed as an attempted assault. As the crook is also hurting himself, a nurse and a supervisor will need to determine if he'll have to be restrained. If he does, then the Tactical boys will enter the cell and restrain him. Thankfully, it's left to the sup to make the call and I'm glad he's the one getting paid the sup's wages.

When the sup and nurse arrive, the sup drops the trap and starts to talk to him, at first receiving no reply. But his calm voice soon gets Dane talking and before long, he's calm enough for the door to be opened. The Tactical boys enter first and cuff him, Dane holding his hands out in front of him compliantly. Once he's cuffed, the nurse enters the cell and does her assessment, the Tactical boys standing close by in case of any sudden moves. The headbutting seemed to have taken the fight out of him as he quietly sits and lets the nurse do her thing. Once she clears him, he is escorted to a desk and interviewed then led to property. Because of his actions, he is only given the bare necessities such as underwear and toiletries. He understands that he'll be transferred to a management unit and will need to remain there until he is cleared for a main stream unit.

As Dane is led out by the Tactical boys a short time later, we continue processing the rest of the crooks; just 4 remaining. It doesn't take long and before we can say "Yahoo, the day is through," the last of the prisoners is walked to his unit, effectively finishing our day. We are all in good spirits as we head out of the building and walk down the corridor towards the front gate. It has been a long day and I can't wait to get home.

"Simon, wait," I hear from behind me and I turn to see Donna Murphy running up the path. Donna is the HR manager and her serious tone raises my pulse a little. As she nears, I can see her face, serious and flat, almost vacant.

"Hey, Donna," I said as she reached me. To my surprise she asked if I could follow her into a nearby building, into a vacant office. Once there, she closed the door and asked me to sit down. The one thing I like about Donna is that she never beats around the bush; straight to the point whether it's a good one or bad.

"I've just received word that Robert Hall has been found dead in his home. He apparently hung himself. Henry Tully was supposed to work with him in Avoca today and when he didn't show, called his neighbour. Apparently the 3 of them know each other. Anyway, when there was no answer, his neighbour let himself in and found him. I know you worked with him yesterday. Did he say anything to you? Was there anything that might have, you know, pushed him over the edge?" My heart sank into my feet as my stomach felt like I'd just swallowed a brick. Images played out in my mind like slow-motion movies as I tried to comprehend her words. She must have seen the shock on my face because she reached forward and squeezed my hand. "I'm sorry," she said. I wouldn't call Robert a close friend but he was a workmate, someone who'd I'd known for a few years and worked with in the prison numerous times. It hurt to hear a man of such incredible experience, end his life because he felt no longer worthy of his place. It made me incredibly sad.

I told her about the previous day's incident in visits and logged into the computer to email her the report. It didn't exactly solve the problem for her but gave her a small indication, especially once I added what he'd said to me. Once Donna had finished with me, she walked me to the door and I walked out alone.

Today, was definitely not a good day.

Thursday, September 27

Rostered day off.

Friday, September 28

Rostered day off.

Saturday, September 29

Rostered day off.

Sunday, September 30

Rostered day off.

The Funeral

Robert's funeral was held a week later and attended by a couple of hundred people. He had spent a lifetime within corrections and I was happy to see so many of his past and present colleagues attend his farewell. Some, like me, came dressed in uniform, and it was very inspirational to listen to the stories many of them had to tell about Robert. Once the church service was complete and Robert had been cremated at the Crematorium, a lot of people attended one of the local bars that Robert used to go to. We spent the afternoon sharing war stories and drinking to the memory of an old mate. I was incredibly sad at how his life had come to an end but will never forget him. To me, he is a fallen hero and one that deserves to be remembered for the years of service he gave. He helped to keep the nightmares behind bars.

I hope you found peace, old friend.

R.I.P.

Robert Hall

June 1st, 1950 - September 25, 2018

Author's Note

It has been another tough month in Maximum Security. But as I write the conclusion on yet another chapter of this series, I look across at the pile of notes I have for the upcoming chapters and can see that there is no slowing down. In store for you in the next Prison Days, October edition, is an attack on an officer that will leave him fighting for life; a Governor's time will finally come to an end; an officer is caught in a very "delicate" situation with a prisoner, and a number of prisoners fall victim to a rather "urgent" problem. The usual assaults, rapes and fights will also feature again and I'm sure you will find October to be as entertaining as the rest.

Thank you again for your continued support and I am always happy to hear from you at prisondays@yahoo.com or on my Facebook page @prisondaysauthor

Finally, if you are interested, I am writing a fictional story based on some of my experiences in maximum security. Join my Facebook page to receive further updates as the project comes to life.

Thank you again for your continued support and I hope I don't ever see you while I'm at work, in a maximum-security prison.

Simon King

Printed in Great Britain
by Amazon